A LOVING GAZE

Edited by

Natalie Nightingale

First published in Great Britain in 2002 by
POETRY NOW
Remus House,
Coltsfoot Drive,
Peterborough, PE2 9JX
Telephone (01733) 898101
Fax (01733) 313524

All Rights Reserved

Copyright Contributors 2002

HB ISBN 0 75432 808 2
SB ISBN 0 75432 809 0

Foreword

Although we are a nation of poets we are accused of not reading poetry, or buying poetry books. After many years of listening to the incessant gripes of poetry publishers, I can only assume that the books they publish, in general, are books that most people do not want to read.

Poetry should not be obscure, introverted, and as cryptic as a crossword puzzle: it is the poet's duty to reach out and embrace the world.

The world owes the poet nothing and we should not be expected to dig and delve into a rambling discourse searching for some inner meaning.

The reason we write poetry (and almost all of us do) is because we want to communicate: an ideal; an idea; or a specific feeling. Poetry is as essential in communication, as a letter; a radio; a telephone, and the main criterion for selecting the poems in this anthology is very simple: they communicate.

CONTENTS

One Single Moment	Colin Skilton	1
A Visit To A Disused Stone Quarry	Arthur Pickles	2
As It Was In The Beginning	Raymond W Seaton	3
In The Gardens Of Villa Borghese	Albert Russo	4
Special Delivery	Brenda Dove	5
Pearl And Lace	Sheila Walters	6
The Day I Grew Up	Janet Fludder	7
Happy In Your Faith	G Buckland-Evers	8
Remember Me	Jane Phillimore	9
Ghosts Of Yesteryear	Brigitta D'Arcy	10
Precious Memories	Francis Joseph Lawton	12
Moving Home	Barbara R Lockwood	13
Sunset	Helen Persse	14
Future . . .	M Courtney Soper	15
Growing Up	Christine Licence	16
Donna	V Barrasin	17
Mother's Word	T M Webster	18
Celtic Heartbeat	Marilyn Hodgson	19
Me And Smugs And A Christmastime Afternoon . . .	Glyn Davies	20
A Fond Memory	Mary Lawson	21
Forests	Kathy Prince	22
The Wonder Of Nature	Berly R Daintree	23
A Visit To Friends	D V Powter	24
I Remember	S J Dodwell	25
A Dash Of Sun	Mair Wyn Cratchley	26
The Calendar	Irene Siviour	27
Magic	F Baker	28
Pure Magic!	Hilary Jill Robson	29
Olde Bells	Roger Mosedale	30
Sweet Morn	H V Bull	31
Special Moments	Jackie Stapleton	32

Title	Author	Page
Hope	Sylvia Goodman	33
Sunrise	Violet M Corlett	34
Aotearoa - Land Of The Long White Cloud	E G Pryor	35
My Moment	Dora Watkins	36
A Faithful Friend	Helen Johnson	37
Listening	Christine Nicholls	38
The Wonder Of It	Ann Bryce	39
Seasonal Changes	Rita Kemp	40
Hot Air Balloons	Catherine Craft	41
The Dress Of My Dreams	Margaret M Donnelly	42
Anna	Jill Dryden	44
Without Words	Michael A Fenton	45
The First Of January	Jackie Warren	46
The Seaside	Derek Pile	47
Chocolate	Susan Carole Roberts	48
Invented Lover	Parveen K Saini	49
Passing Shower	Edwin Page	50
Special Moments	Peggy Briston	51
Heaven's Promise	Lorna Troop	52
There Is . . .	Tracy Tuck	53
Joe	Anne Byron	54
Silhouettes	Jillian Shields	55
Santorini Sunrise	Andrew Cox	56
Millennium	David Marples	57
Best Things In Life	Joan Campbell Jones	58
A Special Moment	Joan Scarisbrick	59
The Beatles Forever!	Christopher Higgins	60
Twilight In Northern Italy	Celia G Thomas	61
Pictures In The Fire	A E Doney	62
Bookworm	Ann Beard	64
My Soldier Boy	J Vessey	65
A Walk With Memories	Jean Paisley	66
Sunset Poem	Sally Barker	67
He Was Born	Wendy Watkin	68
Miss Abigail	Sylvia M Palmer	69

A Day Of Rest	J L Holden	70
Not Alone	Catherine Riley	71
A Fateful Encounter	Lisa Wolfe	72
From One Spirit To Another	Séamas M Ó Dálaigh	73
My Special Moments	Stella Bush-Payne	74
Daydream	Karen Cook	75
Blue Ribbons	P J Littlefield	76
I Love To Cross Children	Lesley J Worrall	77
At Clacton's Cascade Show	Norma Langley	78
JRRT	Hilary J Cairns	79
The Farewell	Alison M Drever	80
Hold The Dream	R N Taber	81
Special Moments	Margaret Findlay	82
The Golden Thread	Pamela Dickson	83
First Kiss	Jill I Henderson	84
Suffolk Pier	Carmel Wright	85
Progress	Audrey Allott	86
Charmouth	Catherine Champion	87
Someone Special	Sylvia Brown	88
First Snow Of Winter	Ann Jones	89
I Love To Write	Vera G Taylor	90
Magic Moments	Kopan Mahadeva	91
Suffer Little Children	Robert Waggitt	92
At One	Jennifer Ramsey	93
Vindolanda	Nicholas Howard	94
Clouds	Evelyn Balmain	95
Alphabet In Rhyme	Leon Gould	96
Harry And Tom	Amanda Jayne	97
An Evening Of Folklore	Tim Sharman	98
Moments	A B Lawson	99
Moments	Dawn Moore	100
Circle Of Love	Jeanne Walker	101
My Love Is Like The First Day Of Spring	C O Burnell	102
An Ancient Story	Kim Montia	103
One Love	Eileen Kyte	104

Title	Author	Page
My First Love	Lorna Neave	105
My First Young Love	Jean P Edwards McGovern	106
Answer The Phone, Give Your Heart A Chance	Elizabeth Martin	107
My Love	Ken Brown	108
Valentine	Stewart Gordon	109
You	A Simpson	110
Love Has Many Faces	Mary V Murray	111
Love	F M Millward	112
Two	Rachael Poyle	113
A True Love	P Wade	114
Desire	Ken Price	115
Love Song	Marjorie Wieland	116
Revelation	Chris Jackson	117
This Is Our Day	Sandra Watton	118
Alone	P W Pidgeon	119
The Sea And Sand	Laurence De Calvert	120
First Love	Beth Anderson	121
My Love For You	Beryl Horwood	122
Before It's Too Late	Jack Karney	123
What Kind Of Love	Carole A Cleverdon	124
Eye Shine	D P R	126
My Love	Mona Pescodd	127
My Love	Fiona Jo Clark	128
In Gold	Pat Mitchell	129
Beautiful!	Graham Mitchell	130
Leah	S Friede	131
My Love	Allan John Mapstone	132
A Shopper's Love Song	Sidney Brown	133
Say Hello	Mark Borsdane	134
February 14th	Susan Wilson	135
Colours Of Love	Helen Posgate	136
My Brief Encounter	Denny	137
Dawn's First Breath	J W Murison	138
Eden	Sue Umanski	139
It Was You	Ato Ulzen-Appiah	140

Through Budding Trees	Terry Davy	141
Loving You	Margaret Bernard	142
Untitled . . . My love it shines	Deborah Hall	143
I Do Love You	Michael Widdop	144
Your Final Port (Will Be My Heart)	Sparky	145
My Love	M D Bedford	146
Time And Time Again	Darren Abbott	147

ONE SINGLE MOMENT

Touch my hear sweet bird of life
That I may fly away until morning
To find my love again
In the coolness of the dawn

Sweet ebony of delight
Ebb and flow through my dreams
To touch and hold me until morning
Turn the water into streams

Time herself awakes me
And rises with the sun
Amid the noise of dawning
Life has just begun

Follow on until the morning
Let the love of life unfold
In the coolness of the dawn
I'm born again

Colin Skilton

A Visit to A Disused Stone Quarry

I walk beneath the gnarled face
and a thousand eyes look down at me;
scattered piles of misshapen stone
and a few earth-clinging ferns
are all that remain of the past.

The wind (a formidable adversary)
clutches warily at this crater
of shattered dreams:

Silence surrounds me,
seeps behind the saddened eyes . . .
wonderful soothing silence
and the deafening roar
of the outside world
fades to a whisper.

Arthur Pickles

As It Was In The Beginning

I started as a microscopic pulse,
A simple vitality before dividing,
Replicating in geometrical progression.
The very stuff of existence,
Becoming fused and firmly locked
Into networks of nerves and individual cells,
Following the in-built blueprint
Of what I was going to become.
Propelled by instincts initiated long, long ago,
When life first exploded on the planet.
An expanding frame formed by coral reefs of bone
Perfectly structured, encased swelling tissues.
My body, inflated as if by some invisible pump,
Lay warm in moistened darkness,
Listening to the comforting thrum
Of a beating parent heart.
Pressure built until I was squeezed
And thrust head first into an alien space,
Where I wailed as I was up-ended and soundly slapped
Amid loud applause following my grand entrance.
Blinding light hurt my eyes, noise pounded my eardrums.
Bathed and safely cocooned in soft warm blankets,
I savoured something akin to dreaming.
Timeless was each slumbering day
Where infant fantasies held sway.
Intuitively, I knew I was unique,
For I knew I was me.

Raymond W Seaton

IN THE GARDENS OF VILLA BORGHESE

the air is cracking
with thunder and zipping clouds
rush of butterflies

the woods are graced with
the statues of foreign poets
abode of lizards

around Pushkin
a Roman family
sets a picnic table

from his pedestal
the author of 'Les Misérables'
stares at a kissing couple

Albert Russo

SPECIAL DELIVERY

'Hello!' I smiled into
Eyes of deep pools
For my heart to float upon.

My son's life begins.

Brenda Dove

PEARL AND LACE

Happy smile upon her face,
Wedding dress of pearl and lace,
Our daughter, a bride to be
A picture of happiness was she.
Hair piled high on her head,
Swopping jeans for this instead!
In her arms a bride's bouquet
Our daughter, on her wedding day.

Doing what page boys should
Her little cousins were so good.
The bridesmaid, doing her best
Adjusting veil and headdress.
The best man, did his bit,
With everyone, was a hit.
Surrounded by friends and family,
Mr and Mrs about to be!
Special moments filled with pride
When our daughter, was the bride.

Sheila Walters

THE DAY I GREW UP

From as early as I remember
I was told to act my age.
What did they mean? I thought at five
As I flew off in a rage.

Aged ten I had some aches and pains,
It's just your age I'm told,
You'll begin to feel much better
When you are twelve years old.

When reaching my maturity
At the age of twenty-one,
At last I may grow up I thought,
But life was too much fun.

I married and became a mum
I must be grown up now -
I've noticed several greying hairs
And furrows in my brow.

When I reached my forties
My mother passed away.
As a tear ran down my cheek
I knew - I grew up that day.

Janet Fludder

Happy In Your Faith

There is a special part of us
So private, and without a fuss.
It bears the roots of happiness,
Away from all the strains and stress.

We feel it deep within our being,
On which the rest of life will wing.
Telling us if we're happy in our ways,
The voice of conscience thus obeys.

With this faith within our childhood,
Protecting us from shifts of mood.
Such inner strength must surely grow,
And will protect from many a foe.

Life on this will then rely,
Protecting us from those who pry.
To keep alive we all must share,
When our whole life will show a care.

This permeates throughout Creation,
And our character will fashion.
Our path in life becomes so clear,
Defending us from every fear.

Then we can see a better world,
Perhaps like knitting row that's purled!
Such bright light will lead the way,
Which we remember when we pray.

G Buckland-Evers

REMEMBER ME

Remember me
When you turn this key
Whether it be
To enter in and
Make that nice hot strong
Cup of tea
Or whether to exit
(Stage left, pursued by a bear?)
Please have a care
And know just how
Completely free
I did become this summer
In your house
Of poetry.

Jane Phillimore

GHOSTS OF YESTERYEAR

A scent of pine
        of coffee, freshly ground
Was that a whiff of
        cigar I could smell?

The candles glowed
        their flickering flames
dancing golden sprites.

The ghosts of Christmas past
        filed silently into the room
and hovered there
        bidding me to remember.

The music we played
        floats through my mind
the sound of a flute,
        tambourines and bells.

Much laughter abounded
        if we sang out of tune
when we could not find
        the notes to Scarborough Fair.

Softly, barely perceived
        I hear the Gypsy Rover
come over the hill
        played on your recorder.

Carols of Christmas angels
        resounded, full of joy
as we ended our concert
        on that day, so long ago.

Still I hear the music
        still I hear the laughter
when the ghosts of yesteryear
        join me in the warmth of Christmas.

Brigitta D'Arcy

PRECIOUS MEMORIES

A family sat on a winter's eve
down by the firelight glow
they sang their songs in harmony
before to bed they would go

Mum and dad
O where are you now my loved ones?
O where are you now in my life?
In countless blooms I most see you
and in memories much treasured
in life. Each flower that blooms I see you
each season it so fills my heart
and with these very precious moments
I know that we are not far apart.

Francis Joseph Lawton

MOVING HOME

Since twenty-two years have passed in one home
Oh how the cost of moving has grown
Agent's fees, search and surveyors' combined
Nobody must be left out of making a 'dime'
Except me of course, I'm not supposed to shine

Why did I succumb to this moving lust
To flee from city traffic was a must?
Noise and pollution, I've had enough
Let me escape to peace and fresh air
Be this, the end product, I've nothing to fear

Packing and lifting, where does one start?
Wish I had someone to give me some heart
'All in a day's work,' a husband says
Tripping over a mat and dropping the bed
Muttering under my breath, 'The last move!' I said

Wondering if we will ever be settled once more
Are my thoughts, as I open a door
To a large pile of boxes covering the floor
Twenty-two years of material wealth
Waiting to be unpacked and placed on new shelves.

Barbara R Lockwood

SUNSET

High on a hill in the east
The sun is slowly sinking;
Streaks of colour across the sky . . .
A sunset of such sublime beauty,
Breathtaking in its wondrous hues,
Reds, oranges and yellows,
Heralding a fine day to come . . .
Or possibly a stormy one.
It brings memories
Of other countries,
But sunsets in England
Are very special.

Helen Persse

FUTURE...

Very high cloud, raining, though don't be distracted
Focus on the work, and then on the beam which
Lights up all directions for one unified sky
Colder, shockingly cold, and then out of nothing
Always back comes the blue and the wind, high rain again . . .

M Courtney Soper

GROWING UP

When your children grow up and your life starts to change,
you forget all those late nights, the tears, joy and pain.
The bumps and the bruises and little cut knees, and holes
in trousers and muddy knees.

The fun and the laughter watching them growing up, wondering what
or where they will be in the year, such and such.
Through the years that have passed and years still to come, you will
never stop worrying whatever they have done.

Whether sons or daughters it's always the same, we try to help them
through the sun wind and rain. Through problems so small, to problems
so big, there's no end to it all, however they live.

They don't realise it now but when they grow up,
we hope they will know they are loved very much.

Christine Licence

DONNA

Did you see the look of joy
That crossed my face that day?
Did you know the love I felt
Or the words that I did say?
Did you feel the tenderness
As I cradled you in my arms?
Did you hear the vow I made
To shelter you from harm?
My love for you is boundless
I give it to you freely
I'll love you always, come what may
I mean it truly, really
I loved you in the early days
Whilst you were still unborn
I loved you even more when
You arrived on that Monday morn.

V Barrasin

MOTHER'S WORLD

Day is velvet soft
as night reawakens

Wind is silk soft
as moon leaves footprints

Silver throated wren calls
grasses whisper in applause

Sunlight glitters diamonds
on bounced rain cobwebs

Autumn leaves fall into sunsets
whilst roseate dawns capture apples

Moon ices winter's nails
that scrape filigree pattern's on windows

T M Webster

CELTIC HEARTBEAT

Fast moving great, grey duster clouds
Harshly polish an already well scrubbed sky
And sigh.
A slogan streaked delivery van
Reading *Pride Of The Clyde*
Throwing up fine spray on the cold, wet motorway.
Curls of sheep dotting soft, damp hillsides
Straying far from grey, stone farms.
Cows confined in lush, milky pastures
By jigsawed, dry, stone dikes.
Pheasants by the roadside stroll
Mists on heather, languid roll
Clouds unfurl, draw shafts of light.
Moon is chased by wind and weather.
Velvety caresses heather.
Skies, like nowhere else can form - slip from grandiose to storm.
And weary kestrels call forlorn
Into the city's orange, sodium night.
Ghostly forms all cast around
On the breathing, steamy ground
Making not the slightest sound.

Marilyn Hodgson

ME AND SMUGS AND A CHRISTMASTIME AFTERNOON IN WELLS

Me and Smugs, driving over to Weston
To walk along a lonely, winter beach.
'How far is Wells?' She asked, smiling.
'I feel that we must go there . . . today!'

Then we were there: in Wells Cathedral city,
On a Sunday, Christmastime afternoon.
Gazing out over our wine, through leaded windows,
Onto a Dickensian, cobbled . . . frosty . . . square.

Strolling through the cathedral grounds,
Into the mighty, ancient place of worship.
Awesome feelings of joy and wonder,
Flooding through our hearts and bodies.

Sat behind the choir at evensong,
These emotions, multiplied by glorious sounds,
Tears difficult to contain their flow,
And moments to remember forever.

Back to our wine, with Christmas card views,
Recalling the lovely past hour.
Soaking up the festive atmosphere,
On this special, Sunday, winter's afternoon.

Home to the fireside, glowing and warm,
Memories to treasure all of our lives.
Maybe next Christmas we'll go back again,
For wine, evensong and olde worlde scenes.

But if it be next year or ever again,
Our memorable afternoon in Wells.
Could never be erased by time,
And we will keep it in our hearts with love.

Glyn Davies

A Fond Memory

In my youth I visited a market garden,
The lady of the house did the flowers,
So you can guess the husband did the rest,
You went down a steep path to get to the front door.

As you went down the path, there, before you,
Stood a whitewashed shed, sparkling bright,
Covered in bold pure purple clematis,
With glorious pink roses cascading through the purple show.

A fantastic sight, unforgettable beauty,
Turn round the corner of the house,
Even more spectacular was the picture there,
Standing straight and tall, three giant thistles grew.

Underplanted by a riot of pansies in every hue,
Their thistle flowers so stately, feeding bees,
Further back was a kaleidoscope of colour,
This was a garden full of love.

Delphiniums, phlox, love-in-a-mist too,
Climbing roses ran up the wall,
The scent of honeysuckle's everywhere,
This indeed was a place to stand and stare.

Whichever way you looked there was something to see,
The tranquillity was overpowering,
This was one lady who had created a piece of magic,
By her knowledge of plants and her endeavours.

Never to this day have I seen anything to compare,
There are gardens laid out to perfection,
Some are made into garden rooms,
Whatever the style, this is the one I won't forget,
Made at a time when flowers were lagging behind
In their availability and a luxury to boot.

Mary Lawson

FORESTS

Forests are a weird and wonderful place,
Walk through them at a slow pace.
Snowdrops, wild flowers and weeds too,
Are waiting to be seen by you.
Sometimes wellingtons you need for there's mud around,
Other times ice and snow can be found.
Tall trees, short trees, some over a 100 years old,
Some stand out looking so big and bold.
Bees, wasps, buzzy flies and now a gnat bite,
Itching away it will keep you awake all through the night.
So many birds, too many to name,
There's some rabbits playing a game.
Insects are there, look at that beautiful butterfly,
A ray from the sun that lights up the sky.
All around the croaking of frogs can be heard,
Chirping and singing from another different bird.
So many pleasant smells mingling all into one,
The day in the forest has been such fun.
The forest is cool and interest it does not lack,
One day soon we are sure to come back.

Kathy Prince

THE WONDER OF NATURE

Capture for a moment the sweet scent of a flower,
The warm aroma of a rose clambering o'er the bower,
The calming scent of lavender running through your fingers.
Carnations, lilies, rosemary, the perfume of them lingers.
What human can produce a fragrance so subtle and sweet?
The perfection of the flowers to God must be unique.

Gaze at all the colours of nature so sublime,
The varied shades of sky and sea, changing all the time.
The glowing hues of sunset skies and the morning sunrise,
The vivid flash of exotic bird as overhead it flies.
Who can produce such colours, so very bright and clear?
Only our God of beauty created colours here.

Wonder at the creatures that swarm the earth and sea,
Amazing the variety wherever we may be.
What wondrous living creatures fill the oceans of the world,
And creepy crawling insects, what mysteries still unfurled.
What human could fathom how to make these creatures live?
God Almighty has the power, all praise to Him we give.

Beryl R Daintree

A Visit To Friends

To glance through chink of autumn light,
The rain green fields and hedgerows sharp
In puddled patterned reflective stare
And skies of uncertain blue,
To fall if threatened, praised or dared.
What gentle treasures of a moment
Hold a memory, recall a fragrance:
Scattered apples, random, brazen, tempting bites,
Sliced and ordered, pie tasty, creamed and dreamed;
And wine and cheese and beans, tomatoes,
In house of pine, full hearted, thankful;
Softly silent whispered history
Of trees, of children, hearts of vision,
Of skills and talent, searched ambition,
Patio bright with sheltered black,
The seasons kindle this visitation.

D V Powter

I REMEMBER

Willow trees bending and swaying,
Breezes gently playing,
Punts gliding on the river,
All send that special shiver
Down my spine.

A bright, sparkling, frosty day
With deep blue sky and shadows at play,
Brown leaves crackling in the crisp air,
When suddenly, smiling strangers share
The warm sunshine.

A phrase of music that rises and falls
Catching the heart, as it recalls
Memories that come flooding by
Like so many birds high in the sky,
All precious and mine.

A word of sympathy, or a laugh,
Cutting problems and loneliness in half,
A look, a letter or touch
Raising spirits, all mean so much,
And I feel fine.

These special moments are all there,
So stop, look, listen and care,
Ignore the pace and noise of life
Shake off the violence, pain and strife
Dream, and share a glass of wine!

S J Dodwell

A Dash Of Sun

A dash of sun where clouds are none,
On fields of green that I've just seen,
Sparkles from the morning dew
Beneath a brilliant sky of blue.

A sprinkle of some summer rain
Makes the green more green again.
A rainbow reaches for the sky
As bluebirds dive and fly right by.

Its colours are of every hue,
Made by the rain where the sun shines through.
It reaches out from fields of green,
Seems like the best I've ever seen.

Clouds that hurry by in vain,
Have only the wind to take the blame.
Soon the moment fades away,
Left is the image of the day.

Mair Wyn Cratchley

THE CALENDAR

I opened up my calendar
The first scene that I saw
Was 'Wharfdale' in its splendour
Transformed in winter white
A beauty so transparent
I'd been here once before

Memories now invade my thoughts
And time was standing still
I reminisce of happier times
Warm feelings to remind
Bringing a sharpness of them and now
Treasuring times of the past

Two people walking hand in hand
Enveloped in love and quiet around
I take advantage - deep in thought
Remembering a sky pink-white with frost
A moment so special we stopped and we knew
That this was forever - a creation so new

As swiftly as life this will all pass us by
But remain untouched as nature reminds
That treasures so poignant made by God's hand
The hills and the mountains
And silver jewelled sands
But now I'll close my calendar and capture once again
Another episode to dream of special moments when
A different place, another time, when I take up my pen.

Irene Siviour

MAGIC

What is a special moment?
A birth, a loss, a gain,
They all have something in common,
In my mind they will remain.
Over the years I've had a few
Some good, some bad, some dear,
But thinking of a special one isn't clear.
I'm married with three children,
And love them all the same,
If I wrote that one was special,
The others would only blame,
So *my* special moment in my life
Was nursing my rabbit back to health,
After being ill and near its end,
This way I will cause myself no strife.

F Baker

PURE MAGIC!

As spring just dawning
I, enjoying morning,
Chilly; as sun held no heat,
Heavy dew spawned, airborne;
Sequin spangled lawn,
Of my hidden personal retreat.

Viewing bulbs new blooms,
Hyacinth scented perfume
Permeating garden moist air,
From floral podium
Of season's blossoms,
Opening dance movement premiere.

Gazing at daffodils,
One trumpet, beyond frill,
Sat an inch-long baby frog,
Drinking clear pearls of dew;
While transfixed I grew,
Awoke knowing indoors I must jog.

Grabbed my camera,
To snap adventurer,
Returned, stooped, ready to click,
Wee frog gracefully leapt
Into white cloudlet
Snowdrops; ballet, nature's pure magic.

A stunning moment,
Cameo enchantment,
Colour captured in my mind,
Seeking sequel each spring
Tiny frog vaulting
To photo, captivate and spellbind.

Hilary Jill Robson

OLDE BELLS

Olde the bells do ring the village round.
Sparkle crowned the snow twizzle
Drinks in the wine sky candlelight.
Mistle hangs within the branch to blotch
The copper penny sun with silhouette.
Crunch the snowfall underfoot with friends.
So soon that moon high lantern rides
With sooty, sparking chimney pots . . .
Carol singing raps the door, iron wrought
As bright inside, merry red and green,
The hollied Yule-log
Rests upon that hotting brass fendered fire.
Christmas pud with cake of plum,
Nuts in mandarin oranged rum.
Snows adrift my winding lanes, about with
Neighbours at the windowpane . . . all jolly.

Roger Mosedale

SWEET MORN

Pastel shades drew violet trace
Our beloved queen fantasia
Shadow of perfection doth breathe
Long shall she grace

Was bound of water lily east of Eden
Where voices of angels whispering
Till morn

Seductive jade exhale this stolen season
Trust she shalt release
Sweet morn

Beneath starry moonlit sky
Reflections of the lady bring

Upon wing of monarch inhale as
Sing
Her lullaby, sweet morn . . .

H V Bull

SPECIAL MOMENTS

Come hold me in your loving arms
Let me wilt to your feminine charms

You're stirring my emotions
You have my ultimate love and devotion

You have opened my heart's closed door
Making it yell, 'give me more'
More of you
Kisses drenched with heaven's dew
Staring at me with your eyes so hazel, so true.

Am safe and warm when am with you,
In your arms.

Held by you.
Am safe and warm in your loving arms.
Here I cannot reset your Heavenly charms those
Lesbian touches we share us two.

We care not what society says we should
Or should not do.

Pure magic is felt after we kiss,
Then a heartbeat felt,
Leaps than missed.

Come hold me
Kiss me,
Make me whole.
Special moment shared between you and me.

Jackie Stapleton

HOPE

There had been no hope.
Last news from Holland
June 1942.
No censored letters
No more Red Cross notes.
Rolling trains across Polish plains.
High smoking chimneys.
The Final Solution.

The tension waned.
There could be no hope
For a Jew
Only deportation
Murder or mutilation.
Cattle trucks to cruel camps
Shivering terror
Then starvation.

Anxiety dulled.
What sense in hope?
A few
Might survive, stay alive
Under cover, quaking
Subsisting, yet buoyed
With determination.

Rewarded hope!
First news from Holland
May 1945.
Well-loved writing
'We are living.'
Heart-wringing emotion.

Sylvia Goodman

SUNRISE

T he unutterable beauty
H olds me spellbound,
E nchanting my very soul . . .

U nutterable!
N o words could describe the magic -
U nutterable!
T o speak would break the spell,
T he peace, the tranquillity;
E llan vannin!
R adiant in dawn's glory;
A dorned with the glinting diadems of a weeping morn;
B edecked in misty grey chiffon,
L ifting and swirling in the fragrant breeze . . .
E llan vannin, little island of dreams.

B lessed am I to behold thee!
E ach new day of my life.
A hungry seagull cries, shatt'ring the silence,
U ndoing the spell . . .
T ime to move on,
Y es, time to start the daily grind.

Violet M Corlett

AOTEAROA - LAND OF THE LONG WHITE CLOUD
(On the beauty of New Zealand, Christchurch, January 2002)

A zenith sun doth blaze the sky,
to cast the clouds in opened eye.

An arc of blue from space is seen,
wide 'neath it spreads a land of green.

Dark-cast shadows the mountains form
to hide each valley ere come the morn.

Snow-capped peaks in silence all sleep,
droplets to shed, broad rivers to weep.

Jet-black caverns bloom with light,
like heavens above that sparkle bright.

Wide plains stretch forth to kiss the shore,
the ocean responds with wave-filled claw.

Forests of beech, silent vigil their fate,
the doe and her foal in stillness so wait.

Fjords sublime, deep secrets they hold
of Tangata Whenua, a people of old.

This land of bounty - for many a quest,
all filled with dreams from east and west.

E G Pryor

My Moment

The final act was over, the curtain had come down.
Then rose again to take the final bow.
The cast were feeling happy, didn't wear a frown
Their minds were on the party here and now
The rehearsals had been hilarious
The first night fraught with nerves
The applause was instantaneous
They got what they deserved
I was quite content
My time had been well spent
The cry of author filled the house
But I kept quiet as a mouse
Out onto that stage I was forced to go
To hear their appreciation of the show
A large bouquet of flowers was placed into my hands
The audience clap and whistle as on their feet they stand
This was my moment, my moment not to share
And nothing and no one can with it compare.

Dora Watkins

A Faithful Friend

A dog is such a faithful friend
He stays close to your side right to the end
Sometimes he's naughty and makes you quite mad
You speak to him sharply and tell him he's bad

He just looks up at you sadly with such a hurt air
Makes you feel guilty; perhaps you've been unfair
However you steel yourself and order him to his bed
And he trots off obediently and lowers his head

But the minute you call him he jumps up with glee
And rushes, tail wagging, puts his paws on your knee
How can you be angry, as smile you must
At such wholehearted devotion and innocent trust

If he thinks you are threatened and feels you're afraid
He responds quickly by barking while rushing to your aid
He's staunchly devoted whether you're neglectful or kind
Devotion of this kind is sure hard to find.

Helen Johnson

LISTENING

Week after week I listened to their grief -
these broken lives, such pain and quiet despair.
I ached to help, but that was not my role -
I gave them coffee, sympathetic nods,
and promised I would pass their problems on
to those who had the power to sort it out.
And when they'd gone I did the paperwork,
wrote up the log and opened up a file
ready for the directors, one would call
and give professional help; and he would send
an ordinary Samaritan living near
to offer long-term friendship, warmth and care.
That was what we did best.

But one dank day
I'd listened half the morning to a man
who poured his troubles out, hour after hour.
Then suddenly he stood, and shook my hand,
'No need to take it further now,' he said.
'You've done a power of good just sitting there
and listening to my woes. And now I see
just what I need to do.'

His shoulders straight
his head no longer drooped, and in his eyes
the gleam of resolution shone. I smiled.
He thanked me warmly, and with sure firm tread
walked from the centre, master of his fate.
And suddenly the day was bright with hope.
Excitedly I entered in the log
'No further action', (oh, momentous words)
my heart aglow with thankfulness and joy.

Christine Nicholls

THE WONDER OF IT

I taught big adolescents
About life and social skills.
Individuals, trying to individualise,
Adhering as they could
To society's norms.
Some listened,
Some rebelled,
Some simply did not care.
But one day,
For a reason which I cannot quite explain,
I held them all in the palm of my hand.
The silence lived.
No word was uttered,
Yet a magnetism, electrified,
Enwrapped us all in private thoughts,
Even though we transmitted in unity, as one.
We all completely understood
The essence of a question asked
So often by the young -
Why?
For one deep magical moment
We felt we knew the answer
In a harmony of fusion,
A comprehension, a knowing.
No one wondered
How we knew
Or why.
It felt right.
It felt good.
Just the once.
Awesome.

Ann Bryce

SEASONAL CHANGES

What a wonderful world in which we live,
where each new season represents a turning point in the year!
Springtime brings hope of fresh new life revealing
bulbous buds, bursting on branches, and
frivolous, frolicking lambs, forecasting
Easter, a special time with its joy, tinged with sadness!

Summer and hot, balmy, relaxing days of rejuvenation and refreshment,
encouraging beautiful, brilliant butterflies to dart around.
The sound of skylarks singing, when swerving and soaring in flight.

Autumn arrives, portraying seasonal mists, carpeting richly coloured
adorned earth; revealing trees which display dripping, dangling,
delicious fruit and berries, which blackbirds strip bare.
Guy Fawkes, Hallowe'en, All Saints, and *harvest festival*,
thanking God for His providence.

Winter, cold, harsh and still, wearing her virginal gown.
The sound of robins, repeatedly rejoicing at Christ's impending birth!
Christmas, that special time, with children's excited, exhilarating
enthusiasm awaiting arrival of Santa and Rudolph,
and the blessed hope of peace and goodwill.
Special moments indeed!

Rita Kemp

HOT AIR BALLOONS

Hot air balloons float o'er my house,
And make me feel small as a mouse.
They fly so high, they look so fine,
Up in the sky, wish one was mine.

I wave to them, I shout with glee,
Can I come too? O, please take me.
My cries unheard, they float on by,
A giant bird, a giant fly.

Where will they go? I know not where,
I'd love to know, I stand and stare.
If I should have a chance one day
To leave this earth and float away,

Amid the clouds, so white and cold,
In my balloon, so brave and bold.
But things like that don't come to me,
All I can do is wait and see.

But I can dream, oh, yes I can,
And I will scheme, I have a plan.
One day I know, one day you'll find,
That I will go, made up my mind.

To scrimp and save, my flight to take,
I'll be quite brave, that trip I'll make.
And then I'll float in my balloon,
O come that day, just come quite soon.

Catherine Craft

The Dress Of My Dreams

It started over a year ago when I joined Scottish Slimmers
I had to lose two stones in weight and cut down on my dinners.
I had to change my eating habits
Stick to three meals every day,
Forget the snacks and sweeties
Not be led astray.

To be honest, it took some doing
I struggled at the start,
But once I got into my stride
It was to improve my health and heart.
The weight came off in ones and twos
Which really is quite perfect,
And when Mary rang her bell
I knew I'd reached my target.

I gained a new self-confidence
I no longer felt a frump,
And compliments from my friends
Meant I was no longer plump.
The time had come for a new image
A short hair cut was the first to change
And next it was the wardrobe
A more up-to-date fashion range.

We had a New Year party coming up
And I wanted a stunning dress,
It had to be really sparkly
And better than all the rest.
I shopped around with my daughter
We covered so many shops,
And I was about to give up
When I saw what was to be my frock.

It was made of soft smooth black velvet
With glitter starbursts by the score
I had found my dream creation
It was my special moment, could not wish for anything more.
When I wore it to the party I cannot remember feeling so good,
It's all down to Scottish Slimmers and me
For keeping a sensible eye on my food.

Margaret M Donnelly

ANNA

When illness strikes someone whom you love
You take guidance from above
When Anna took ill she couldn't walk
She couldn't move but still could talk
She was only three, what could we say
We had to wait and we did pray.

She's started to walk and move her hands
And on her own, she can even stand
On her splints are flowers of pink and blue
And physios show her what to do.

Her wheelchair is her carriage now
But hopefully soon it will take a bow
For Anna the days are looking brighter
And for me, her granny, so much lighter.
Friends have showered her with so much love
Thank you dear God for being above.

Jill Dryden

WITHOUT WORDS

The mime dancer choosing
the most focal point of the park
displays his art,
explodes any thoughts
of humbling himself.

The gyrating movements
in yin and yang
encompassing his needs,
sacrificing the tranquillity
by flaying and scything
his imposed arena
to demonstrate his will
to be obeyed - in triumph -
like a chainsaw in a silent forest.

A passer-by stood in wonder,
by shadows hidden,
his silent form moved
witness to betrayal.

The seed to flower,
to fall a seed again,
but felled in the act:
the air drowned all hearing,
the soundless fall betrayed again
that moment in time when -
neither did he cast a shadow
nor was a shadow cast upon him.

Michael A Fenton

THE FIRST OF JANUARY

The streets are silent now.
I could walk forever,
seeing the world
through fresh eyes.
Breath billows white,
each intake stabbing
the lungs like
shards of ice
despite the sun.
Here and there
broken bottles,
empty cans;
remnants left
by last night's
revellers
still cheering
the twelfth stroke
when a year's ghosts
had been laid to rest,
old acquaintances
forgotten
and new ones made
in a haze
of cigarette smoke.

Jackie Warren

THE SEASIDE

Maybe to sit awhile
To watch and breathe the sea,
Seagulls on food sorties
Soaring on the winds so free.
The chill October breezes
Hurt the ears, blow the hair,
But, to enjoy the seaside
Does anybody care?
Walking along the Esplanade
Just drinking in the view,
Laughing at people's antics
Surprised at what they do.
Those mad or brave in the water
Paddling in its chill,
Young children on the sands
So amazing their thrill.
Out across the water
Boats sail on through,
Their spirit of adventure
Amazing but nothing new.
The place out in the distance
Where cliffs stand up brave,
To the ferocious wrath of the ocean
Every beating destructive wave.
I could go on forever
Taking in this wonderful day
But it's time to make our move
Not just sit and stay.

Derek Pile

Chocolate

A quiet moment
a chocolate moment,
like time melting in your mouth.
A velvet moment
a dark chocolate moment
that melts and then heads south.
Brandy liqueurs, whisky creams and
Cointreau flavoured nectars
inside a delicious chocolate shell.
There's orange, coffee, cherry and strawberry
centres to feast upon as well.
The delicious flavours that nuts
all add to chocolate too.
Chocolate covered brazils, whole hazelnuts,
and walnuts in a whirl, with toffee praline, oooh.
All covered in that scrummy chocolate
made for me and you.
But what can be better
in the hot weather, than everybody's dream,
that's right, a long cool refreshing . . .
chocolate ice cream . . .

Susan Carole Roberts

INVENTED LOVER

To meet as strangers today
On the other side of the road.
It's been so long, let me touch your lips,
Oh I have longed for . . .
I remember your face but name not known.
Please don't apologise for ignoring my existence,
You were only part of my dreams, my invented lover.

Poems of the past, which described your beauty
Seem quite ordinary now.
The poems are worthless,
But still hold a special bar around my heart.
Loved one, you may laugh the poems off,
As I have cried myself to sleep many times.

Kiss these poems and let them die.

Parveen K Saini

Passing Shower

The rain begins to fall
Upon the sound generator,
The clear plastic roof,
Conservatory becoming a chamber of noise
As the pattering becomes persistent,
A chaos of confused tapping,
All drops blending in both sound and form
As the roof becomes awash with water.

A new rhythm begins,
Tapping louder,
As a drop from the roof above
Falls regularly, heavy and laden;
The bass drum to the myriad snares,
All marking the passage of the clouds above,
Which go unseen as we shelter inside.

Edwin Page

SPECIAL MOMENTS

Wind roared as it swept on its boisterous way,
So inside by the fire I decided to stay,
Watching the boughs in the storm shake the trees,
I was glad to be home, but was suddenly seized
With a burning desire to be out in the snow.
Thoughts of winter deterred me, but I had to go
The desolate land called me, and urged me on,
All sense and reason now suddenly gone.
The snow was cruel and whipped at my face,
Why was I trapped in this desolate place?
Home and warmth such a short distance away,
But I was compelled by some force to linger and stay.
And then I spied it, a flake of white snow
Etched on a rose leaf growing below
A magical pattern growing apart
A wonder of nature, a work of fine art.
A filigree snowflake so perfect and rare
I could only marvel, just stand there and stare.
A delicate petal of water and ice
Each one was perfect, I knew in a trice
Why I was forced to this magical place
To feel the cold snow and sleet on my face
It imprinted the glory of God on my soul,
I'll remember it always, wherever I go.

Peggy Briston

HEAVEN'S PROMISE

Walking through rainbow
colours and bridging
misunderstandings
friendships rebuilding.

Warming in brightness
minds and hearts changing
casting out darkness
hope reawakening.

Weaving the seven-fold
shades purely blending
peace, love and mercy
gently enfolding.

Waltzing the vibrant
colours and soaring
gliding in Heaven's
promise enduring.

Lorna Troop

THERE IS . . .

There is . . .
No clock,
nor traffic light or boardroom.
No deadline,
no car
or artificial light.
There is . . .
Stillness that ripples,
strokes pebble and shell,
retreating and returning,
day and night.
There is . . .
Green and blue,
water and rock.
Seething with life
raw and sweet.
There is . . .
It fills,
and I am complete.

Tracy Tuck

JOE

Warm as a hot water bottle,
The child, a vulnerable bundle,
With knees tucked up, arms crossed,
Snuggles into my chest.
Cheeks milk-bloated,
Head pushed into my neck,
Face pressed onto my shoulder.
He breathes in slow monotony.
Large searching eyes closed,
And cheeky, cock-eyed grin
Relaxed into peaceful confidence,
He tugs at my heartstrings.
Does he know, our Joe
That he's stolen his grandma's heart?
A wisp of a smile - or wind -
Flickers across his face.
Disarmed by his innocent charm,
And memories of maternity,
I savour the moment
. . . And Joe sleeps on.

Anne Byron

SILHOUETTES

I remember the soft crunching
of the shell-strewn pebbles
beneath our numbing feet
that late autumn day.

Our scarf-wrapped souls
linking arms as the gentle
lapping of the sea seduced us
with its liquid harmonies.

Red-tinted noses shining from
the sinking sun, the faint
plunging of distant stones
thrown by laughing children.

Leaning on your shoulder as
the salty wind whipped my
hair across my glistening tears,
watching the boats return.

The smell of the seaweed
garnishing our brown paper bags
of fish and chips as the lights
on the pier came out to play.

The soaring seagulls with
black wings against the
blazing sky, bobbing and
dropping like the shadowed boats.

Feeling your woollen hands
cupping my rosy face,
your lips on mine. Still, I feel
those warm hands,
that late autumn day.

Jillian Shields

SANTORINI SUNRISE

Early morning, in solitude, I stand on the beach
Black ash surrounds me, sands of time measuring infinity
Silhouetted against a greater picture
An orange, peach glow
Marks the beginning of the day
I wait and wonder . . .

My thoughts race to the vision
Of countless others who too have stood here
Ancestry of thousands of years past
This is my place in time, but we are united in one
They too must have come here, to think, to ponder over their fears
For you are the same light.

I gaze across the inky waters
Slowly you rise over the horizon, where sea meets sky
Rays streak into the air, a fanfare of light
To mark the coming of a king . . .
Your crown appears
And I wince at your power.

Inky blue turns to gold, shimmering light, reflections on waves
Like a night sky with a million twinkling stars
Sea and night sky, are one
And still you rise
I feel your heat on my skin, it tingles with anticipation
Of full beauty and splendour to come.

Fully risen, a great fireball, medallion of the skies
You bellow in brightness
A thunderous roar of unsaid word
'I am the light of the world'
King of stars and prince of light, Isis, Apollo
Darkness is defeated, a new day is born.

Andrew Cox

MILLENNIUM

The new millennium was celebrated by all,
Down our street and over the wall.
Rockets thundered into the sky,
Some people went round asking why?

Whistling fireworks went up on high,
All the colours of the rainbow went by.
People all over the world awoke,
Many said that it was a joke.

Different resolutions are made as a sign,
Making promises to keep for all time.
After all the merriment is done,
We are all looking for some fun.

For all the time we are on this Earth,
We do what we can no matter the worth.
One thing for sure is the moon and the sun,
We will not be around for the next millennium.

David Marples

BEST THINGS IN LIFE

What I have gained knowing you
How trustworthy and understanding
How you'd cared for me
To me you were a special person
I'm proud to have known you
Because you were my husband.

Joan Campbell Jones

A SPECIAL MOMENT

I'd been away,
A time to rest,
A time to think,
What's for the best?

A time to relax,
A holiday in the sun,
No pressures there,
Away from everyone.

I came home,
Not knowing,
Until that moment,
With face glowing
And arms outstretched,
I saw you -
And then I knew!

Joan Scarisbrick

THE BEATLES FOREVER!

From the early raw energy days of Hamburg to Abbey Road,
timeless lyrics and music, and a sense of humour, flowed,
first as the Quarryman, the Silver Beetles, and the Beatles now,
young talent from Liverpool, thrilling a new generation, and how,
Penny Lane through to Strawberry Fields, a portrait of the Queen,
whatever the era or decade, misunderstanding all that is seen,
John Lennon, Paul McCartney, Ringo Starr and George Harrison,
this quartet - the fab four, two of these are sadly gone,
ten original years of excitement, a breath of fresh air still,
since the tragedies of 1980 and 2001, chance of reforming was nil,
with Brian Epstein as a manager, and George Martin producing,
creating euphonic sounds where instruments and vocals sing,
Beatlemania, something never before seen, reigned long and supreme,
Merseybeat inspiration, came at the right time, born of a dream.

Christopher Higgins

TWILIGHT IN NORTHERN ITALY

Low clouds, like fine-spun hammocks flung
Across the evening sky,
Gave gauzy shelter from the sun
And blanked its fierce eye.

They ebbed and flowed in measured mode
Like billows on the ocean,
Massing over Venetian hills
With silent, leisured motion.

But the full glory of the sun
Burst through magenta haze,
Colouring cloudlets red and gold
In one majestic blaze.

Then shadows fast and furious
Followed us as we sped,
Racing through lingering twilight
Now that the day had fled.

The spotlit castles seemed to be
Suspended in the air,
Like cut-outs, one-dimensional -
No earthbound contact there.

Soon the glories of Lombardy,
Caught by the thieves of light,
Surrendered all shape and substance
To grasping shades of night.

Celia G Thomas

PICTURES IN THE FIRE

Early twilight trims the lamp,
carefully across the cattle-ramp.
Fetch wood to wake the dusty hearth;
pass Michaelmas daisies up the path.
Pale stars which autumn hoped to prolong,
faded their yellow hearts all gone.
The wind has blown countless down,
and every centre turned to brown.
Once galaxy of amethyst,
ghost faces risen in the mist.
Mauve visitors which have no say,
for wilful winter forces his way.
I watch the sea-smooth driftwood burn,
blue smoke and scent of far return.
Sparks spattering the chimney throat,
red molten motes of sunken boat.
Fate is written in the flames,
forgotten ships, lost lives, unnamed.
The heartbreak clang of warning bell,
loud, then fades, above the swell.
White surf aboil, wild torturous snakes
pounding to death, the ship's heart breaks.
Broken masts, torn, tangled shrouds,
from craft the owners once were proud.
Gale shrieking devil voice from Hell,
smash vessel like a brittle shell.
The fearful crunch, the dangerous list,
sad phantom cry 'Abandon ship.'
I am the dreamer by the fire,
toss Michaelmas daisies gust snapped spire.
Shape storm wrecked ships in burning wood,
surfed shoreline, waving natives stood.

And dancing, leaping in the flame,
a pretty, dusky maiden came.
Swirl tropical water, warm moon dipped,
I woke with salt upon my lips.

A E Doney

BOOKWORM

My books are my friends,
The answer to my prayer.
Ones full of laughter,
Excitement one can't compare!

Books of knowledge and education,
Facts and figures to define.
With guidance and support,
Adds foundations to time!

Some with moving parts,
Music, to ring out the words.
Nothing hasn't been thought of,
Anything crazy goes, how absurd!

Cloth and plastic pages,
Card, with metallic print.
Books a comforter through time,
Answers that help us think.

My favourite book is mine,
A log of time gone by.
Of achievements and experiences,
Special unto me, till I die!

Ann Beard

My Soldier Boy

On my forehead he placed a kiss
It was a kiss that I would miss
He let go of my hand
He turned, he frowned
And picked his gun up from the ground
And walked away without a sound
Off to his duty, war-wards bound.
I watched until he was no more
Felt the parting to the core
As my tears began to pour
I tugged my sleeve until it tore.
No words did pass from him to me
His lips were sealed, they had to be
And I was left in purgatory
Wondering would again I see.
He was a man, but once a boy
But always a boy in a mother's eye
Time was cruel and slowly spent
Well-wishers called with good intent.
Then I heard this wondrous sound
Approaching boots on gravelled ground
And on my forehead he placed a kiss
It was a kiss that I had missed.

J Vessey

A Walk With Memories

Hill all fresh and green like ample maidens
laying on a couch,
your scent pervading noses of both human
and the beast.

All things of hoof and wing sing out a
chorus on the morning air,
the water lapping over stones as tiny
fish make bubbles on the top.

Cathedrals of dark trees they tower
with barks knurled, thick as any pillar,
flat green squares where men and women
bowl black glossy balls.

Wire bending, still tall round flat courts
that used to harbour students in short skirts,
square red brick pillars and concrete floor
once fountains of fresh water seemed to
flow forever more.

Strong planks, old railway sleepers, bridges
made with metal rails now hang across the streams,
dogs all bark and children scream when
rain beats down upon the scene.

Jean Paisley

SUNSET POEM

Watching the sun fade - brings me back to you
sleeping on my shoulder
warming my body as you warmed my soul

The sailboat on the sun-filled horizon
driftin' further out of view
Memories cloud my eyes
as I squint to keep up with it
not really wanting to see beyond that horizon
Not yet

I need time
sun don't set completely, warm me one more day
wrap your rays around me
let me understand the rhythms of your change

Teach me to go down gracefully
with peace and beauty
but remaining an integral part forever
sinking slowly into the water losing myself,
shadows - but remaining forever
Together as one

Sally Barker

HE WAS BORN

Christmastime when we were young
And Father Christmas came
The stocking lay heavy - we mustn't peep,
But Ann did, all the same.
'A book! A torch!'
'Sssh go to sleep.'
'It's only three o'clock.'
The bells in the sky were ringing,
. . .He was born . . .

A star was shining bearing the news
And people flocked to see -
Such a long way away from us
. . . He was laying . . .
. . . He was a King . . .
Mary was tired, Joseph was proud
As they looked at the smiling crowd.

We pushed our shiny new prams
With two identical dolls.
We had dinner with our gran
As the holly hung brightly red.
News was spreading rapidly
. . . A King of Kings is born.
. . . A King to save us from sin . . .
On this - this special morn . . .

Wendy Watkin

MISS ABIGAIL

Abbey the birthday girl,
Your birthday fell in August,
A very much wanted child,
How you kept your mummy waiting,
In fact you drove her wild,
Just one day old - in your little cot,
Right by your mummy's side,
I knew you were a child of God,
And in you - His love abides.

The cutest little cherub,
Of this - there was no doubt,
Perfect little fingers, and little rosebud mouth,
A gift from Heaven - beautiful in every way,
You brighten the lives of a certain little family,
Each and every day.

And look at you now, a child of three,
Sitting on your daddy's knee,
You radiate such love - and your love to us never fails,
We all adore the charming - happy, mischievous
Miss Abigail.

Sylvia M Palmer

A DAY OF REST

When I was a girl, Sundays
were a day of rest with the
family. It meant wearing
the best dress, white hemmed socks
and black patent shoes.

Going to church was a must
where the preachers in the
pulpit on high, shouted about
our sins, of the Devil and Hell.
Then we sang with gusto hymns
of God and His love.

Then home to Sunday lunch
we would go, where Father
carved the joint, and mother
served the veg, when we'd had
our fill, off to the kitchen she
would go.

While Father, the master of
the house, sat in his big
armchair with Saturday's
newspaper, and after a little
while a gentle snore could
be heard, while I sat with
hands on lap, waiting for
Monday's washing day, after
the day of rest that was so special.

J L Holden

NOT ALONE

Sometimes it seems, when life gets tough,
and the way ahead is steep and rough,
then, it seems, we walk alone.

When apprehension, doubt and fear
alienate us from all that we hold dear,
then, it seems, we stand alone.

When the heart is sad, and love is no longer blind,
and reason admits false images of the mind,
then, it seems, we grieve alone.

Yet when a sister stretches out caring hands,
and our brother assures us He understands,
then, it deems, thank God, that we are not alone.

Catherine Riley

A Fateful Encounter

We only met when we were past our prime
After each severed marriages from former time.
We met up in a crowd and quite by chance
Came face to face. He asked me to dance.
There was a spark, not yet a burning flame
We made small talk and asked each other's name.
They call me George he told me with a smile
I liked that name; we chatted on a while
And made arrangements to go to a pub
The next week after visiting the club.
And soon love blossomed but there was a hitch
We each had children to look after, which
Made it impossible for us to have a chance
To be together, had to postpone our plans
Until nearly three years had passed
And then his daughter married - when at last
We too had our wedding day, to live as one
Till death did part us, twenty-nine years on.

Lisa Wolfe

FROM ONE SPIRIT TO ANOTHER

Even in the mists of drink it was
an aggregation
of spirits
non-metamorphosis
of minding
each the other's
sensitivities
playfully capriciously
she with him
tenderly unexpectedly
he with her
in the presented
moment
foraging new ground
childlike keenness
of reciprocation
inexplicable unsought
unveiling
of a breasted secret
unsolicited
before this night
mutualized now
leap of
soul
hand
eye
imbibed poetically

Séamas M Ó Dálaigh

My Special Moments

On waking, when I see the sun
That has to be my number one,
It peps me up, fills me with glee
The sunrays bring me energy!

My loving cats, one, two and three
Come around purring, greeting me,
When the postman drops the mail
It's my number two and three I hail.

When a poem 'acceptance' I receive
It's a *special moment* you must believe,
This would be my number four
And who could really ask for more?

Stella Bush-Payne

DAYDREAM

Tears from a candle fall
Fragrance touches the wall
Music gently embraces the room
As I let my imagination consume

Galloping horse so wild and free
Thundering hooves under me
Spraying sea and sand wedges
Nuzzling leaves as we clear hedges

A setting sun with rose tulle
Fading light by a rock pool
Wandering along a deserted beach
Autumn rides and solitude reach

A lover's hand calm and still
Amongst the sand dunes until
You say goodbye to summer's charm
To be together arm in arm

Karen Cook

BLUE RIBBONS

Special moments fill my memory,
Well they seem special to me,
My memory is one of the only bits of me that now works OK,
Can't button my shirt or go for a walk,
Can't tie my shoes or burn my toast,
I have to rely on others for everything,
Now all I can do is remember and quietly talk,
So all my memories are special moments,
Like when I flew down the wing,
Cut inside and scored from twenty-five yards,
My team mates hugged me and we won the cup,
I can remember clearly when first I saw my wife,
She now lives up in Heaven,
We first met when I lived at number nine,
She and her family moved into number seven,
That was nearly sixty years ago,
But that moment is still crystal-clear,
She wore a red dress with blue ribbons in her hair,
She smiled and said hello,
I knew then I'd never let her go,
So no matter what my future holds,
I still have my dreams,
I tell anyone who will sit and listen as my story unfolds
About my life, my hopes, my past,
My listeners often smile and drift away,
Leaving me muttering away to myself,
It's in the lap of the gods how much longer my conversations
And my life will last.

P J Littlefield

I LOVE TO CROSS CHILDREN

I love to cross children . . .
See their tender smiles
All weathers . . . Church days,
Watch their cute, fun ways
At Assembly or see work in classroom displays.

First I wore a police badge
I served faithfully,
Responsibly . . .
'Please walk carefully
Unkempt shrubbery.'

This brow, wide junction
Teaching me lessons,
I carried my heavy
Lollipop stick all those years
Burdened by known fears.

That willow tree too
Held mysteries for me . . .
Memories taunted,
My past confronted
Clearing points of view.

The bulbs freshly bloom,
Daffodils, crocus
Brighten in springtime
Daisy-filled parkline
Where history looms . . .

As I visit of course
I have a lump in my throat,
Remembering when . . .
I wore that bright coat
And cross children again.

Lesley J Worrall

At Clacton's Cascade Show

A magic moment in the show
On which eyes and ears could feast.
When Andrew Robley rendered
'Beauty And The Beast'.
A most moving performance
With a misty atmosphere,
Romantic, tender, magical,
A memory to hold dear.
Two misty dancers in the background
Andrew's deep expressive voice,
His apparel adding to the scene,
It made my heart rejoice.
Of all the other lovely songs
This stood out from the rest,
Andrew sang romance, strong and true
For me, this was the best.
My experience lives on in me
Never shall I forget
The way I feel about that magic
Lingers with me yet.

Norma Langley

JRRT

Just when I'd plunged to the depths of despair,
Unable to find solace anywhere;
When it seemed that there was nothing for me,
Then into my life came JRRT.

As he made me feel like a child once more,
I fed on his works with rapture and awe;
I felt the excitement, I felt the fear
Of Legolas, Aragorn, Boromir.

I hungrily feasted on ev'ry line
As I proudly followed the chosen nine;
But my hunger grew harder to assuage,
Ever increasing with page after page.

For I was a part of that stalwart band,
Facing their dangers with sword in my hand,
Sharing the deeds on this dangerous quest
Of Gandalf and Frodo, Sam and the rest.

Their adventures never ceased to enthral;
Wholly consumed by the thrill of it all
I was transfixed as if under a spell
By the magic and charm of Rivendell.

I urged Frodo on when he gave up hope,
Dragging myself up Mt Doom's awesome slope;
I held my breath as he clung to the ring
Whilst I willed him on to do the right thing.

For a while he let me inside his head;
I shared his thoughts with each page that I read;
I'll cherish those moments reverently . . .
Those moments I spent with JRRT.

Hilary J Cairns

THE FAREWELL

Her eyes dancing with laughter, she smiled as she waved goodbye,
as she had done many times before.
I waved in return until she was out of sight
as I had done many times before.

I did not know then that I was bidding her farewell
and would never again see her loving smile.
Lord, the memory of that last farewell
I treasure more than words can tell.

I thank you Lord, for your gift of visual recall,
imprinting the image of her smiling face on my mind.
May this picture never fade that I can keep alive,
the memory of her loving friendship, encapsulated in her smile.

Lord the memory of that last farewell
I treasure more than words can tell.

Alison M Drever

HOLD THE DREAM

World, collapsing all around;
Skylark, winging without a sound;
Sweeter memories, like a kite
tugged free from precious hands
at Nature's whim;
Lights in the eye grown dim;
Candles in the soul, flickering
like shadows on a blind;
Mischievous sunshine, out of sight,
out of mind;
Suddenly, sounds of children
playing in the park invade our dark
and lovers' songs who pause
to watch and share - dreams
of a future together;
And where are you, but here?
And who am I, but blind with despair,
to let you drift like a lost kite
tugged free from precious hands
at Nature's whim?
Forever, lights in the eye grown dim
shall flare, candles in the soul
grace the altar of true love,
our lives on wing,
singing . . .

No kite a sweeter memory
or lark's lay such ecstasy.

R N Taber

SPECIAL MOMENTS

Our hotel room was just perfect,
And the view made it complete,
Before us was the deep blue sea,
Sky and mountain seemed to meet.

Each day I longed for evening,
To watch the sun go down,
For the colours were so rich,
Like jewels in a crown.

The sun itself, a huge red ball,
As it dipped into the sea,
The clouds displayed their colours,
It was an artist's fantasy.

Then suddenly the sun had set,
And darkness came instead,
But a yellow moon and one bright star,
Shone down upon my head.

If I had been an artist
That scene was made for me,
But I know forever in my dreams,
That picture I will see.

Margaret Findlay

THE GOLDEN THREAD

The little child shone like a light,
An aura she had that was so bright,
An angel that had lost its way,
From a different sphere that had gone astray.

Through her veins the lifeline flowed,
Pure and untainted, like liquid gold,
The thread of her being, so strong and fine,
Nothing could destroy the power divine.

It attached itself to her soul,
The thin gold line, until she was old,
The golden thread was her existence,
With it she could run any distance.

Like a flower in the rain,
This child withstood all the pain,
The golden thread was her rod,
For she was guided and touched by God!

Pamela Dickson

FIRST KISS

For a while we were friends walking the dog
Laughing, talking, having platonic fun.
Gossips thought we should not be a couple
But as time went on the affection grew
Feelings changed. One night we followed our hearts.

The moment we kissed the world stopped turning,
Stars were pulled to a vacuum round my head.
I felt my heart jump from my chest to yours
Universe gasped! We could have fuelled comets
That energy has never stopped flowing.

Jill I Henderson

SUFFOLK PIER

Miss Daisy takes the air along the pier
A fine June morning, clear and cobalt blue
With such a flutter in her tightly buttoned breast
A new be-ribboned bonnet
Perched upon her upswept hair
Light step, white parasol aloft
Soft rustlings of her satin skirts
Along the boarded, slatted floor.

A wooden rail . . . she leans and looks
And ah! she spies the little knot of men
Spreading out, long loping strides
Along the sand, coat tails flying,
Heads held back, loud laughter,
Voices carried by the wind.
He's here, he's here, below her, unawares,
Dark, handsome, charming Billy boy.

Carmel Wright

PROGRESS

When I was young my talents were few
But as I became older my talents grew
So varied are they now, painting and computing too
Swimming, poetry and dancing I like to do
Is it a talent or hobby? You be the judge
It takes me out of myself and makes me budge
I guess it's because I now have the time
To spend how I like, be it painting or rhyme

Audrey Allott

CHARMOUTH

Strong fresh breeze blowing off the sea
While the sparkling waves come tumbling in,
Pure clear light dazzles half-closed eyes
As we stroll 'neath the cliffs as a warm day begins.

We sit down on the steps by the smooth wet sand,
Watch our small child play in a pool on the beach,
Absorbed in the sounds and the feel of the day,
Who said that true happiness is out of reach?

Catherine Champion

SOMEONE SPECIAL

I have never had a friend that was true,
Until I met you.
You don't think of just yourself,
For you help others too.
Not for what you can get,
But what you can do.
You help lift their spirits,
When your own is maybe down.
There are not many people like you around.
There was only one that I knew,
But he is dead and gone.
I hope that in me his spirit lives on.

Sylvia Brown

FIRST SNOW OF WINTER

Softly the snow falls to the ground,
Swirling gently, without a sound.
Fields and meadows with a covering of snow,
Forming drifts as the winds gently blow.

Frosted patterns on the windowpanes,
Diamond icicles in country lanes.
Snow clinging to the trees and bush,
White wonderland lays in a hush.

Cobwebs white, like delicate lace,
Fine as the veil, covering a bride's face.
Virgin snow surround the lake,
Liken to icing, on a celebration cake.

Ann Jones

I Love To Write

Writing is something I love to do,
Using my skills to send out to you
A message full of love and cheer,
Or it could be a simple prayer.
Sometimes I am full of inspiration,
However, there are times of frustration,
When the words are locked inside my head,
But then words come when I am in bed,
I'm wide awake, I cannot sleep,
Into the office I have to creep,
For if I had to wait until morning
The words would vanish with the dawning
Of the new day with so much to do,
There aren't enough hours for me and you.
But after all my sweat and pain
It has not really been in vain.
So a very special moment for me
Was when a publisher did agree
That the words that I had written
Were beautiful and full of inspiration.
I knew that God had helped me through
To send my words out from me to you,
This was a special moment of mine,
One which only my God can define.
So never give up, use your pen
And you'll get things published now and then.

Vera G Taylor

MAGIC MOMENTS

The first vision of our first-born dolly
Seen in *scannoscopy,*
Showers of snow on Christmas eves
When weathermen swore there wouldn't be any,
Receiving refunds from the revenue gods
Unasked, unexpectedly,
Hot baths and beers before the screen
After gruelling days of drudgery,
Cheers and applause from audiences
When I recite my poetry -
These are some gem-like magic moments
Ingrained in my memory.

Kopan Mahadeva

SUFFER LITTLE CHILDREN

Suffer little children to come unto me,
the words of Jesus so we all could see
His love for the children.

How do we teach the children to know the love of Jesus?
We tell them the Bible stories every passing year,
but do they really believe the Christian words they hear?

Look to the Bible and you will see
a commandment from Jesus made to you and me.
'To love one another as I have loved you,
and they will know that you are my disciples'.

The corner stone of our faith is love,
so look for guidance from above.
And teach our children well, the reason we love Jesus so.
Do the children really know that Jesus loves them too?

Is Sunday school just a place to be
while the Christian grown-ups recharge their batteries?
What Christian input do the children receive
on this Sabbath day?

Ask a child and you may hear the truth of the matter,
what do they know of Christian faith?
Is it only what we grown-ups say,
or does the holy spirit move a child in a special way
we adults cannot understand?

For it's only as children can we enter the gates of Heaven.

Robert Waggitt

AT ONE

Emotions stripped bare, we stand before each other.
Souls naked, exposed but safe, no judgements.
Complete respect allows this extraordinary time.
Mutual trust, mutual understanding, kindred spirits united.
Deep unconditional affection exists;
And yet I am confused by the strength of my feelings.
Let not society judge me with a label of how or what I feel.
Do not be afraid of these words, no additional baggage do they bring.
I can find no other expression but this, purely and simply;
I found I loved you.

Jennifer Ramsey

VINDOLANDA

The red squirrel darts his secret way
The owl has told the hours of the night
Till thrush and blackbird, finch and robin wake
And bid it end its vigil for the dawn
A ground mist hangs voluptuous in the air

Rabbits stop; alert to every sound
And sheep watch their newborn lambs
Vigilant in their defencelessness
A hoar frost whites the pasture and the wood
Vigorous but delicate on the fells

No people yet; and quiet still prevails
The caressing whisper of a westerly breeze
In harmony with the gurgling of the stream
Though spirits of the place are stalking here
Theirs is a noiseless haunting

This is no easy place
Desolate and bleak the resonance is there
Of Pict and Roman screaming in their wars
The clash and thud of sword and spear and axe
The lust for death that typifies mankind

Today no windswept rain
No woman wails nor soldier gasps in death
No violence on earth but gentle mood
A beautiful seduction and deceit
For Vindolanda whispers 'it is spring; trust me; all is well'

Nicholas Howard

CLOUDS

Clouds heaped high to far horizons,
With golden nimbus edging grey;
Castles looming over chasms,
Streaming blue pennants for the fray.
White sailed galleons floating high
Across the heavens' vast ocean;
And sable horses, riderless,
Charge swift in high winds' motion.
Nor ever is the scene the same
Its shapes and colours changing fast;
Nor ever does the artist tire
Till all the panoply has passed.

Evelyn Balmain

ALPHABET IN RHYME

A is for awareness, what we are here for
B is for beauty, the things we adore
C is for charm, God's gift to each
D is for our dearest, those within reach
E is for ever, God's love to you
F is for family, a brotherhood so true
G is for God, who sends out His love
H is for Heaven, where He resides above
I the individual, you and me
J is for joyful, happy and free
K is for kindness, to love and behold
L is for love, the petals unfold
M is for mother, who nurses with care
N is for nature, her beauty we share
O is for old, to grow old with grace
P is for purity, it has its own place
Q is for quiet, in holiness we abide
R is for regal, in God we can confide
S is for serenity and calm
T is for talking, our interests so warm
U is for united, our hope for world peace
V is for victory, for all wars to cease
W is for water, earth's precious mineral
X is for excitement, when friends assemble
Y is you, these things you can do
Z is for zeal, of all things true.

Leon Gould

HARRY AND TOM

If I had to place the very best moments in my life
It would be the very days I gave birth to you both,
                              not being anyone's wife

Every day I love, just witnessing the funny things you both do
Things are taken for granted in this life, but nothing on earth
                              will ever shake my love for you

Amanda Jayne

An Evening Of Folklore

The clear blue beauty of the voice
That can make the heart rejoice
Folk songs about John Barleycorn
Jack in the Green in his shifting form
Stories of country folk living fully
No time for the mechanical bully
To think about nature and ourselves
Old leather-bound books on dusty shelves
To understand nature and live with it
Not to destroy and ruin all of it
The girl's voice penetrates the soul
Some of us in the mist looking for a role
A part in the play as seasons change
Songs pour out in fullest range
Legends and centuries weave
Through the long grass and leaves
Leaving a single person enriched
The carpet of the seasons fully stitched.

Tim Sharman

MOMENTS

A moment has gone
And a moment has come
A moment is lost
And a moment won
A tick is a moment
All round the earth
Forever passing
And giving birth
Living and dying
A breath and a sigh
A laugh in a moment
A moment to cry
A moment in sailing
A moment we drown
A moment that saved us
To renew us around

A B Lawson

MOMENTS

Special moments are to share with someone
It's something for us to cherish
It's a feeling that you belong
A time which you can relish
Mixed emotions rolled into one
A memory you have forever
It's something that's been done
A moment you will endeavour.

Dawn Moore

CIRCLE OF LOVE

I love - the moment when I wake,
The magic light that heralds the dawn,
The wondrous chorus of wild birds.

I love - the feel of dew on grass
As I walk barefoot through the fields,
With rising sun to warm my back.

I love - to feel your lips on mine,
Hear how your heart beats when we kiss
Before you softly say goodbye.

I love - to watch our sleeping child,
The warm damp hair clings to his brow,
I kiss his cheek to waken him.

I love - the friendly creaking gate,
Your footsteps on the gravel path,
Your voice as you call out 'Hi! Love.'

I love - the circle of your arms
As we lie quietly waiting sleep.
My greatest love of all is you.

Jeanne Walker

MY LOVE IS LIKE THE FIRST DAY OF SPRING

My love is like the first day of spring
It bursts forth fresh and tender
And every hour renews itself
With passions I remember.

Your beauty dear can never fade
Although the years may flow
For I see you only through the eyes
I looked through long ago
So on my heart a note is pinned
If I die before you do
Remember my love is in the wind
Always caressing you.

C O Burnell

AN ANCIENT STORY

Spun, the thread of self-deception
Shimmering by candlelight
Lies run sweet at their conception
Dripping honey through the night

Murky waters of desire
Swallowing my strong resolve
Rising steady, ever higher
Feeling all my doubts dissolve

Smell the scent of morning glory
Fumbling with thoughts anew
Crying out an ancient story
Though the words are very few.

Kim Montia

ONE LOVE

My love for you will never die
And some days I can't help but cry
For I know you will never know
Just how much I love you so
I first saw you many years ago
But was too shy to even say hello
You would pass me by without a glance
I should have known I didn't stand a chance
But I was young and had my dreams
And they lasted well past my teens
Sometimes I wonder where you are
And if you have travelled far
I wonder if you passed by my way
Would I still recognise you today
Like the song says, 'First love never dies',
And I know my tears will never dry

Eileen Kyte

My First Love

My first love came into my life unexpectedly,
turning it upside down, making me realise
I could change my life around.

He gave me a great happiness in my life
and I was filled with utter contentment.
We would go for many walks on long sunny lazy days
and talk and talk and smile as our many talks
led us to walking down the aisle.

My first love taught me the precious gift of love and loving,
to love someone is to have a sense of purpose and responsibility
to protect and care for this person as if they were
as precious as life itself.

To love and be loved in return fills my heart
with the utmost happiness and blissful contentment.

As for my first love, we've survived the trials and tribulations,
and enjoyed many celebrations,
for my first love stands beside me still,
and we treasure our love for each other and always will.

Lorna Neave

My First Young Love

We met and fell in love, at the age of nineteen
So carefree, and innocent, a love through our teens
I will never forget my very first love
Which will always remind me, of a little white dove

When walking in the park, watching the squirrels play
And the cooing of the dove, courting on a fine day
As the birds sang sweetly amongst the trees
Their leaves seem to whisper, against a light breeze

When strolling hand in hand, through the summertime
Those days will always remind me of a lovely rhyme
A rhyme that puts words together, just like a melody
So sweet a sound like music, bringing the sweet harmony

As we danced around the buttercups, and clover
Such magical moments, that we shared with each other
Love-light shone in our eyes, as we shared a kiss
Still, I dream of those times of loving bliss

Such blessedness, we knew till the sun disappeared
Parting with another kiss when the twilight appeared
Still, I think of my first love in a special way
As though those days were just yesterday

Each weekend he would take his leave, from the Barracks Square
A guardsman to be proud with, with so many things, we did share
After two years of courtship, I just let him depart
Through young foolishness, and such a foolish heart

Whenever I think of those golden hours of love's dream
Just like music, that dwells within, like a lovely theme
To dream yet once again of my first young love
Which reminds me, so of the flying first little white dove

Jean P Edwards McGovern

ANSWER THE PHONE, GIVE YOUR HEART A CHANCE

Her heart beats fast.
Her head hesitates; it does not approve.
Self-sacrifice, her head declares it right.
Heart rails against head; it can feel her spirit diminish.
Heart finds a supporter and leaps with joy on hearing its needs voiced.
Her heart beats fast.
This time heart has to win . . .
Answer the phone!

Elizabeth Martin

MY LOVE

And is my love as steadfast as the rock
That juts its granite into swirling seas?
Or fickle as the clouding April sky
That sheds its raindrops in a warming breeze?

And when the polished satin of your skin
Has faded with the ravage of the years
And when your eyes, so bright with fledgling joy,
Are dimmed with age or washed with pain-filled tears,

And when your form, so lithe with youthful strength,
Sleek as the otter, swift as a young gazelle,
Is loose with age and worn with grinding toil,
With tell-tale marks and infant-bearing swell . . .

And when no more the music of your voice
Soothes and restores my soul and heals my fear,
And when my fingertips no more longer thrill
To touch your cheek or smooth the silk of hair,

How will I love you then in autumn years,
When russet tints usurp the emerald shades?
How will I love you then, in darker days,
When young desire has fled and beauty fades?

Yet I would pray that love endures and lives,
That when the flames of passion flicker low,
A gentler, yet consuming love will stay
And prosper in the embers' dying glow.

Ken Brown

VALENTINE

You are my Valentine,
You are the only one,
No longer will I stand
Alone, beneath the sun.
Instead of which I find
That you are by my side,
So let me take your hand
As we both go through life
And to the land beyond.
You are the only one,
You are my Valentine.

Stewart Gordon

You

The way you look at me and smile
Somehow you make it all worthwhile
Being in your arms in the dark night
You know it feels so very right.

I'm glad I've got you babe
It's so good to know you're mine
I'm glad I've got you babe
Stay with me for all time.

Smiles in sunshine, tears in rain
Laughter, sadness, pleasure and pain
We hold hands and tenderly kiss
Feeling good in our loving bliss.

When I get tired you know what to say
To ease and cheer me, you light my day
When I feel lonely, I can turn to you
With you at my side I'll never stay blue.

I'm glad I've got you babe
It's so good to know you're mine
I'm glad I've got you babe
Stay with me for all time.

A Simpson

LOVE HAS MANY FACES

Love has many faces,
Portrayed in many ways,
Stirs fire within the coldest heart,
To melt the hurt away.

The love of man for woman,
That denies all humankind,
A mother's love for her children
That lasts throughout her lifetime,
Growing stronger day by day,
Each tugging at the heartstrings,
Then eddying away.

The love of life achievements,
Weathering of the storm,
Grip of life held on to,
That makes a person strong,
Love of those remembered daily,
You lost along life's way,
Held deep down within one's being,
Forever there to stay,
Love of sheer contentment as,
Autumn years unwind.

Mary V Murray

LOVE

I have loved you truly,
It seems like yesterday,
When you walked into my life,
And took my breath away.

You gave me something,
I had never had before,
You gave me a special happiness,
You made me love you more.

Thank you for the months of love,
Thank you for loving me,
Thank you for coming into my life,
And showing me what love could be.

And as I tread along life's path,
I know I will be sad,
But I will always remember a special man,
Who once made me so glad.

F M Millward

Two

I watch him sleep.
Eyelashes flutter childlike.
His arms snake silently around my waist.
And he smiles, slowly, sweetly.
I stroke his cheek.
Eyes smile, unconsciously,
And I cannot imagine another happiness such as this.
He makes me feel so protected and so warm.
So protective and at peace.
I breathe in his complete adoration and wrap myself in the knowledge
That together we are perfection personified.
Every thought is joy.
Every word is love.
And every number is 2.
It's with him I love to spend my days, my hours, my life.
To sleep and walk, to laugh, talk, cry and eat.
It's with him I am complete.

Rachael Poyle

A True Love

Before you came into my life
Everything around me was dark and cold.
But now I don't feel lonely
Now that I have you here to hold.

I'm going to break these rusty chains
That keep me shackled to the past
Because in you I've found true love
And a love that was born to last.

I want to see the old boy smile again
So I've got to take a hard look at me
I'll even give up my hopes and dreams
If it's the way things have to be.

It feels like I'm going home
And that I've finally found my way
I've found a home in your heart
A treasured place where I can stay.

I'll sacrifice a lifetime in Heaven
If that's what I have to do
I would spend my days alone in Hell
To spend one last precious day with you.

P Wade

DESIRE

The day struggles
to its feet,
attempting to bandage
its deepest wounds -

The blood continues
to flow.

Dark, now,
the sun - has not yet
risen
over the graveyard.

Death pollutes
the beauty of summer
in the long grass.

Where are you?

I search for you
in the summer rain.

Your voice -
your smile -
the touch of your hand -
the gleam of your skin.

Then - I find you
forever certain,
solidified
behind my eyes -
warm, glowing, yielding,
to my -
desire.

Ken Price

LOVE SONG

It is a joy to me
To be with you every day.
When you are there
You make my morning.
It is filled with brightness
And the day is easier.

I hear your steps
And the place where you are
Is filled with music.
Who else makes my heart sing?
Who else but you
Is music to my soul?

Marjorie Wieland

REVELATION

This force is spontaneous
Feeling of total attraction
Passion, desire
Physical sensation
That grows with intensity
Creates a glow
And you just know
It is love
Because
The magical footprints
Remain on your heart
Imprinted
Spring to life
Whenever together
Frolic mischievously, invisibly
Dressed in lace so serene
Courting
Light as air
Merging
To totally share
Without a care
For a moment in time
Amongst the clouds
In space.

Chris Jackson

THIS IS OUR DAY

Today is our day
You're looking rather well;
I see you glimpse
Across the room
But not me you see.

I caught a little teardrop
As you turned to me and smiled,
My heart felt rather heavy
But only for a while.

You, quietly whispered in my ear
I had to say goodbye,
For now and forever babe
It's only you and I.

Sandra Watton

ALONE

There'd be no falling tear,
If you were near,
No more an empty sigh,
With you close by.
This sweetly scented air
We both might share,
Watch moonlight on the trees
Spread by the breeze,
Whilst sky, cloud swathed
Now all in silver bathed.

But beauty's sway
Is lost with you away.
You need not strive
To keep my love alive.
For you would know
How deep this love's aglow.
So hold your trust,
If you feel you must.
You would not doubt my vow
Were you here now.

P W Pidgeon

THE SEA AND SAND

Her hair is like the sea
It can be wild and tempestuous
It breaks over my fingers
And knuckles
My hands swim in it
As I search for the bones
Of her seascape.
Often I can feel a soft
Reassuring breeze hit my face
As we become one
And sand and sea fuse
Into bands of multipurpose
Rhythms.

Laurence De Calvert

FIRST LOVE

Love lay in a quiet corner of my heart
until you came along

Now my heart leaps with the light
the light that shines
when your eyes meet mine

Awakened like the meadow flowers
with their first flush

Beautiful and fragile
like the birth of first love

The precious thoughts of you
soothe me like crystal drops of dew

The winged seeds of love have taken root
and blind youth bear the stolen fruit

Floating on an apple blossom cloud
amidst showers of soft pink petals
the hungry hearts of youth
revel in love's festival

The harvest moon spills out her beams
the love bird sings
enticed by the ripened fruit
we love, and go on loving
unaware the haunting fragrance of fate
is forever waiting in the wings

Beth Anderson

MY LOVE FOR YOU

I cannot find words to say how much I love you
I love the earth beneath your feet and the skies above you.
It doesn't matter how near or far
I just have to be wherever you are.

There is an ache in my heart
Whenever we are apart.
To me you are so very dear
I only come alive when you are near.

You are my perfect lover
I'll never want another
You truly are my best friend
To all my wants and needs you lovingly tend.

If I ever lost you my world would be dreary and dark
If you ever left me my world would fall apart.
These words can never tell you how I really feel
All I know is that my love for you is everlasting and oh! so real.

Beryl Horwood

BEFORE IT'S TOO LATE

Tell her you love her
And want her to be in your life forever
That she is God's very own daughter
Who came to save you
By her presence
At the eleventh hour of a terribly bleak day
That her breath of fire keeps warm
All the dreams and desires
That were dying beneath the ground she walked on
That she is all you lived for in those dark and desperate days
And all you keep going for
During the harshest of hard times
Tell her
That you love her
Those words that in retrospect came cheaply
Now
Mean nothing less
Than the world

Jack Karney

WHAT KIND OF LOVE

Unrequited all consuming
Passion that runs high
A song of love sang softly
Words that say 'I love you'

Hold my hand, soft and gentle
Caress my hair, bath in my eyes
Hold me close my precious one
Sleep contented by my side

I dream of you, fond thoughts I keep
What name will I give to you
When I see your face
Will I recognise you?

I do want you to find me
Wherever you may be
By the light of the moon
When stars are bright
I'll see you then my love

This heart I have
An organ of fire
Burning just for you
Passion that will flame

Come home to stay sweet love
Hold me close my darling
You are my only love
Stay here . . . don't go, it's only me

I am a lover and a friend
There is no bargaining for my heart
It's free to you sweet love
Sleep deeply my love, don't go

We will be together
In the sun, just you and me
Our soft and gentle love
My own special one

Carole A Cleverdon

Eye Shine

i love to see the twinkle
that shines within your eyes
those special little crinkles
that revel that you are mine
if in people's company, at the floor it's best to look
because they may decipher and interpret the glance
if we looked our eyes would lock, and so the inevitable trance
the trance that leads to longing, which turns into a kiss
a kiss that leaves all cares behind, responsibilities forgotten
a kiss that leaves all time untied, adrift on our passion
so now the die is cast, and what will be will be
together through the thick and thin, that's how all love should be
so over shoulder, to see that no one sees
I will look as you will look, forever fervently . . .

D P R

MY LOVE

'Twas magical for both of us when first we met and fell in love.
It felt like all the stars in heaven were shining from above.
His kisses were so tender as his arms he held around me,
I really was in Heaven where I longed to be.
Hoping this would last forever, just for he and me.
The magic of the tingles running up and down my spine
Had me in a tizzy, exclusively mine.
Love gives you a wonderful feeling, of this there is no doubt
And when you have found your true love that's what it's all about
For love conquers all.

Mona Pescodd

MY LOVE

you're my love
you're my sweet craving
my holy dove spirit rising

and i'm praying
for the sanctity of our love

i want you to
wake me in the morning
kiss me without warning

and miss me so
whenever you are away from me

should the moon
lose its place in the sky
should all the stars fall
and the rivers run dry
should the rose cease to bloom
and pigs with wings fly

my love for you would never alter
never falter, die but be forever true
for it is constant, continuous and self-renewing.

Fiona Jo Clark

IN GOLD

No, I don't need just now
to be beside you in your tousled bed.
Alone on this sun-warmed grass,
caressed by light, dazzled
by buttercups, I'm happy
in my body, as my body dreams
of you.

A mood of afterglow
and, stunned by grace, I trace
the gently curving corners
of your mouth, while eyes
smile into eyes; or kiss
the summer sky of freckles
scattering the long, gold
symmetry of your back
and catch my breath
remembering how we found each other.

Warm winds bend the grasses.
I'm shaken
by that deep-down joyous laughter
that seems to overtake us
after love. This is a moment
of purest bliss. I feel no need
to have you here with me.
Bathed in your love
as surely as in sunshine,
alone and together are the same.

Pat Mitchell

BEAUTIFUL!

Beautiful!
Julie is beautiful!
Like the birds sing,
In the morning.
Julie is so beautiful!

Beautiful!
Julie is beautiful!
Like the flowers,
In the garden.
Julie is beautiful!

Oh!
She's the girl,
I've been longing for.
The girl I simply adore.
I'd be lost without her!

Beautiful!
Julie is beautiful!
Like a sunset,
On an evening.
Julie is so beautiful!
So beautiful!

Graham Mitchell

LEAH

Every cloud's lining is silver
And I'm gonna love her till the
Stars no longer shine!

I've always wanted to be a star
Sing my songs, play my guitar.
Since I met Leah I know I'll go far
For she means the world to me!

Leah has a beautiful face
A sexy smile, a warm embrace,
Since I met Leah I can stand the pace
For she means the world to me!

Leah means the world to me -
Her tender touch is ecstasy!
I know she will always be
The only girl for me!

Fondest feelings, deep inside
Tender love that's hard to hide
Prevented by my foolish pride
From singing my love for you.

Darling how I love you so
You'll never know how deep
So let me whisper in your ear
The secret you must keep.

Every cloud's lining is silver
And I'm gonna love *you*,
'Til the stars no longer shine.

S Friede

MY LOVE

Love can come at any age
It is all the rage
It can come at any time
When you sip or when you dine
On a mountain top
Or at a bus stop
It can strike
When you are on a bike
Like a magician who waves a wand
Love at first sight is a bond
Some may part and go away
But they will come back another day
You feel you have known them all your life
In happiness, joy and in strife
In your heart
You know you will never part
My love told me her birthday was the day after Valentine
It was then that I knew she would be mine
We had many years of love and bliss
Her I will always miss
I remember vividly the day she died
I screamed and I cried and cried

Allan John Mapstone

A SHOPPER'S LOVE SONG
*(with acknowledgements to 'A Subaltern's Love Song'
by Sir John Betjeman)*

Sweet check-out Sue, sweet check-out Sue,
Witty and pretty, my heart aches for you,
The endless piped music, the race down the aisle,
To 'Under Ten Items' and your gorgeous smile.

So happy to help, so willing to serve,
How mad I am, sad I am, steeling my nerve,
Your cheerful chit-chat, your voice warm and true,
I'm weak from your loveliness, sweet check-out Sue.

What speed at the scanner, such beautiful eyes,
Those nimble slim fingers that tot up my buys,
Your soft auburn hair, if only you knew,
Cupid's arrow has struck me sweet check-out Sue.

Nine-forty, ten-fifty - to hell with the cost,
My knees start to tremble, all dignity lost,
As I proffer my money our hands lightly brush,
I feel my pulse race, my face gets a flush.

My heart's fit to burst, my trolley is too,
It's chock-full of goodies, not one of them you,
A faltering look, unable to cope,
I make for the exit - a tryst my last hope.

Informed that you finished at just after eight,
I sit in the car park and patiently wait,
You've hugs for your husband when he collects you,
A receipt I am left with from sweet check-out Sue!

Sidney Brown

Say Hello

Sultry in the summer,
Sitting straight beside me,
But on your left,
So you did see,
The sparkle in my aphekic eye,
Which was only for you,
And that is right,
There is no other in my view,
Only you. In the winter
When we did not meet,
I was left 'out in the cold',
You stood 'on your own two feet'.
Smiling in the spring,
Sitting straight before me,
Not to the left, 'Hello,'
Lest we lose opportunity,
To hold each other,
In this hot summer,
As is right
My dark and sultry lover.

Mark Borsdane

FEBRUARY 14TH

The card that I hold in my hand
Breathes colour and life and is grand
Hearts and flowers tell me that you are mine
My one and only Valentine.

And flowers arrived at the door
The colours, more than a score
The card says I am divine
And again you say I am your Valentine.

But who are you? There is no name
Did you leave me once, to return again?
Or did I meet you on holiday?
There is no name, you do not say.

I am divorced, I have no lover
Disabled too, my life near over
But to know you think I'm divine
Causes the sun to shine
Thank you, my Valentine!

Susan Wilson

COLOURS OF LOVE

White is the colour of pure love, innocent, blameless,
Unspoiled like virgin snow.

Pink, the blush of puppy love, the kind we all have known,
Painful in its awkwardness.

Red, a fiery passion that burns within the breast, driving
Some to forbidden fruits, which always taste the best.

Gold, dripping honey, sweet nectar on soft, moist lips,
Sensual and passionate, a wealth of treasured bliss.

Yellow, as in summer sun, warm, happy, smiling,
Light on your feet, glad to be living, life is sweet.

Green, eyes of jealousy, watchful, suspicious mind full of
Distrust when it raises its ugly head, true love is surely lost.

Blue, is when love breaks your heart, pain so real stabs
Your soul, will it mend now you are both apart?

I have worn all these colours at some point in my life, now
Black adorns me in grief, I cry in a cold empty bed.

Mourning our love, days and nights that will now never be,
You never said sorry, when you walked out on me.

It came so unexpectedly; I could not take it in,
The way that you hurt me was really a sin.

In my grey empty life, I exist only to love you
Basking in memories, the colourful afterglow.

Helen Posgate

MY BRIEF ENCOUNTER

I didn't know it then but you were my 'brief encounter',
The gamut of emotions I held down, the smile without the laughter.

I couldn't tell you then but I was in Heaven and Hell,
Together side by side in that waiting room in a timeless spell.

The train arrived, we both got on, knowing this was our last journey,
The Heaven was your nearness, but I couldn't touch - you weren't free.

I couldn't tell you then the pain was too much, this was my Hell,
I felt you knew my unspoken pain, I felt your suffering as well.

I held so much back then, it's locked deep inside,
I wonder do you still keep a place where you hide.

A time capsule that leaks now and then 'exquisite pain',
That bitter sweet memory that last day on the train.

So many things I wish I'd said that you will never know,
I should have told you how I felt, knowing you must go.

Of how I needed you to stay and what you meant to me,
But I was young and quite naïve and couldn't let my words run free.

So here I am and much too late to ever put it right,
If you'd stayed and shared your life the chances were we might.

I'll never know the might have been, the what if, or the maybe,
To have built a life together and perhaps create our baby.

I didn't say and nor did you suggest that we hold fast,
Instead we let life divide and rule and shut us in the past.

With all we both had locked inside we should have faced it
                                                         hand in hand,
It seems that 'brief encounter' was the most that life had planned.

Denny

DAWN'S FIRST BREATH

Dare I compare thee to dawn's first breath
That gentle kiss of sunlight against my naked chest
Your gentle caress, morn's first breeze
That fills me with life as gentle fingers tease

Still darkened grasses blow
Your silken hair cascades and flows
The petals that open with sun's first kiss
Your sweet perfume, heavenly bliss

And in your eyes a shining light
Night's last star twinkles bright
With lips as fresh as morning dew
Every kiss a pleasure new

Dare I compare thee to dawn's first breath
Yes

J W Murison

EDEN

Forbidden as you are,
You remain forever potent.
And I cannot regret,
Every stolen moment.
For a love that is not free,
To be given or received,
Is the longest and the hardest,
And the one that's always grieved.

Sue Umanski

IT WAS YOU

We fought the ups and downs of life
Life is a stage and
I thank heavens I got to know you
But love at first sight wasn't a clue
Since you were in a web
Bound by many like you
Your voice is like molasses
One that the sober
Takes and craves for more
Your beauty is like art
One that the painter
Creates till he can do no more
You brought joy into my life
And I realised love was alive
And you led me to my dreams
To the reality of imagination
Because I never envisaged
Such immaculate architecture
Your smile is like the sun
As bright as white light
You invaded my impregnable fortress
And brought honey to my tongue
I had not tasted such sweetness
Since my breasted birth
When true love is above
When every wave we crave
Is out of this world
You brought meaning to my vision
And it couldn't be anyone
Than my true love

Ato Ulzen-Appiah

THROUGH BUDDING TREES

When the sun does dance through budding trees
And the swallow soars on summer breeze,
My heart will skip a beat or two,
My eyes will shed a tear for you.
As all good things in life, like these,
Bring back the memory of you.

When winter bites and takes its toll
Then I will weep and pray for your soul.
The pain of never seeing you again
Is too great a lifelong strain.
But bear we must till life, I trust,
Will offer its harvest of nature's best
And follow the path of all before
That walked this earth or nature's shore.
For who knows when the final wave may come
To take one more that merely died
Back to our greatest pal and friend
On the final ebb of life's last tide.

Terry Davy

LOVING YOU

To be happy is to share
each day with you.

To know the true meaning
of wealth is to experience
the richness of your love.

Every hope,
every dream fulfilled
in loving you.

Margaret Bernard

UNTITLED

My love it shines
Straight from the core
Darling
It's you
Whom I adore
With tender kiss
And warm caress
Your precious heart
I now do bless
These arms of mine
Are meant to hold you
Let love's embrace
Now enfold you
Whilst angels keep
A watchful eye
Together again
You and I.

Deborah Hall

I DO LOVE YOU

Come now my dear
Let's raise a cheer
A glass or two
For you
Of sparkling wine
Bubbling so fine
A friend or two
By you
Raise up your glass
Let's join the class
The night is new
For you
Champagne it is
Oh! Not to miss
This royal do
With you
But morning hails
As night time pales
A splendid view
Of you
I see your face
So full of grace
And so it's true
I do love you

Michael Widdop

YOUR FINAL PORT (WILL BE MY HEART)

If life was not worth living, I'd still try to make you live
If you were unforgiving, I would teach you to forgive

If the years were just too boring, I would make the boredom go
If all you want's adoring, I'll be there to let you know

For when there is no glowing, I will always be the spark
The strength behind your growing, the sole candle in the dark

Turn to me for comfort
When you feel like turning in
I'll be the final resort
When you feel you cannot win

For so often I had dwindled, not expected to come back
Yet with courage you rekindled me and put me on the track

Regrets once crossed my memory, I did cross that turnstile too
At a point in time I couldn't see that I was losing you

And now you need my comfort as the days are turning in
Let my spirit be your escort for together we will win

Turn to me for comfort
When you feel like turning in
My heart will be your final port
Your home, your love, your yearning

Sparky

My Love

My love first came together
When I was only three
My baby-sitter sat me
Down and on her knee
My love then gave me comfort
So I shed not a tear
For I had had a nightmare
My love took away all fear
But my love got married
Oh her blossoming joy
I am just four now
To my love's pageboy
Yes my love, I held her hand
Even walked her up the aisle

M D Bedford

TIME AND TIME AGAIN

Time and time again,
The thought of you plays on my mind.
A whole day's thought is spent on you,
Thinking how my love is true.

Time and time again,
Words flow as freely on paper as they do in my heart.
In my mind we can't be apart.

A secret from my past holds me back.

Time and time again,
I picture you clearly in my head.
Capturing each word you have ever said.
Too afraid to speak out loud,
My feelings on paper break through the cloud.

Like brilliant sunshine in the morning sky,
My love for you will never die.
Amazed by you walking down the street,
Hoping that our hearts will meet.

My heart beats faster when I see you smile,
I capture that moment, but just for a while.

The urge to see you every day,
Means no excuses and no delay.

Now I feel our love is near,
I hope that what I have written stands out clear.

Darren Abbott

SUBMISSIONS INVITED
SOMETHING FOR EVERYONE

POETRY NOW 2002 - Any subject,
any style, any time.

WOMENSWORDS 2002 - Strictly women,
have your say the female way!

STRONGWORDS 2002 - Warning!
Age restriction, must be between 16-24,
opinionated and have strong views.
(Not for the faint-hearted)

All poems no longer than 30 lines.
Always welcome! No fee!
Cash Prizes to be won!

Mark your envelope (eg *Poetry Now*) **2002**
Send to:
Forward Press Ltd
Remus House, Coltsfoot Drive,
Peterborough, PE2 9JX

OVER £10,000 POETRY PRIZES TO BE WON!

Judging will take place in October 2002